50 Decadent Soup Recipes

By
Brenda Van Niekerk

ISBN-13:978-1503001954
ISBN-10:1503001954

Content

Almond And Herb Soup 7

Artichoke And Potato Soup............................8

Asparagus Soup..9

Barley Mutton Soup 10

Bean And Macaroni Soup...............................11

Bean And Pork Soup.......................................12

Bean Sausage Soup 13

Bread Soup...14

Cabbage And Tomato Soup............................15

Caper Soup...16

Cauliflower Soup 17

Chestnut Soup..18

Chicken Cheese Soup 19

Chicken Chowder 20

Chicken Noodle Soup 21

Chicken Vegetable Soup 22

Chili Butternut Soup.......................................23

Clam Chowder..24

Coconut Soup With Rice 25

Corn Chowder..26

Crab And Corn Bisque 27

Crab Soup..29

Creamed Spinach Soup 30

Cream Of Tomato Soup..................................32

Cullen Skink Soup 33

Curried Pumpkin Soup 35

Fish Chowder 36

French Onion Soup...37

Hungarian Goulash Soup...39

Lentil Soup 40

Lobster Bisque Soup Recipe 41

Mango Soup...43

Mushroom Soup 44

Onion Soup 46

Parsnip Soup 47

Pea Soup 48

Pea Soup With Dumplings..49

Potato And Sweet Chili Soup 50

Potato And Zucchini Soup 51

Rice Soup...52

Rice And Onion Soup 53

Salsa And Black Bean Soup 54

Scotch Broth..55

Seafood Chowder...57

Squash Soup..58

Sweet Potato And Lentil Soup..60

Tomato And Basil Soup 61

Vegetable Soup 62

Zucchini Soup 64

Zucchini And Apple Soup 65

Almond And Herb Soup

Ingredients

187 ml almonds (finely grated)
1500 ml chicken broth
750 ml fresh cilantro
500 ml fresh parsley
187 ml cream cheese
12,5 ml fresh oregano leaves
12,5 ml fresh marjoram leaves
250 ml shrimp (cooked and de-veined)
Slivered almonds for garnishing

Method

Combine the almonds, 500 ml of the chicken broth, 375 ml of the cilantro, 250 ml of the parsley and the cream cheese together in a blender.

Blend until smooth.

Transfer the mixture to a saucepan.

Add the remaining chicken broth.

Simmer over a low heat for 20 minutes.

Combine 250 ml of the soup, the remaining cilantro and the parsley and the oregano and marjoram in a blender.

Puree until smooth.

Combine the puree and the soup in the saucepan.

Add the shrimp.

Simmer for 3 minutes.

Garnish with slivered almonds.

Artichoke And Potato Soup

Ingredients

1 lb artichokes (washed, cleaned and chopped)
1 lb potatoes (peeled and chopped)
1 onion (peeled and chopped)
1 quart water
1 oz butter
5 ml ground black pepper
10 ml salt
1 pint of milk

Method

Combine the artichokes, potatoes, onions and water together in a saucepan.

Cook until tender.

Add the butter, salt and black pepper.

When tender remove from the heat.

Rub the mixture through a sieve.

Return the liquid to the saucepan.

Add the milk.

Bring to the boil.

Add water if the soup is too thick.

Asparagus Soup

Ingredients

24 sticks of asparagus
2 pints water
5 ml ground black pepper
10 ml salt
1 pint milk
50 ml corn flour
1 oz butter

Method

Combine the asparagus and water together in a saucepan.

Boil until the asparagus is tender.

Add the salt and black pepper.

Combine the corn flour and milk.

Add the milk mixture and the butter.

Bring to boiling point.

Stir constantly.

Boil until soup is smooth.

Barley Mutton Soup

Ingredients

1 kg mutton (cubed)
250 ml barley (rinsed)
2000 ml water
4 carrots (peeled and chopped)
2 onions (peeled and chopped)
4 sticks celery (sliced)
1000 ml beef stock
10 ml salt
5 ml ground black pepper
15 ml fresh parsley (chopped)

Method

Combine the mutton, barley and water together in a saucepan.

Cover the saucepan and cook for 90 minutes.

Add the carrots, onions, celery and beef stock.

Cook until the vegetables are soft.

Add the salt, black pepper and parsley.

Bean And Macaroni Soup

Ingredients

125 ml baked beans
62,5 ml onions (peeled and chopped)
6 ml garlic (minced)
250 ml tomatoes (skinned and chopped)
62,5 ml macaroni
10 ml corn flour
5 ml oregano
25 ml cream
25 ml tomato ketchup
25 ml butter
Salt to taste
1000 ml hot water
25 ml cold water

Method

Sauté the butter, onions and garlic together.

Add the baked beans, tomatoes, macaroni, salt and hot water.

Once the mixture is boiling allow the mixture to simmer until the macaroni is cooked.

Dissolve the corn flour in the cold water to form a paste.

Add the paste to the soup.

Add the oregano, cream, tomato ketchup, salt and pepper and mix well.

Bean And Pork Soup

Ingredients

1 lb dried beans (soaked in water overnight and drained)
10 ml salt
1 onion (peeled and chopped)
3 ml ground black pepper
2 lb pork ribs
1500 ml water
187 ml BBQ sauce

Method

Combine the soaked beans, salt, onion, black pepper, pork ribs and water in a crock-pot.

Cover the crock-pot and cook on Low 10 to 16 hours.

Remove the ribs from the crock-pot and cut meat from bones.

Return the meat to the soup.

Stir in the BBQ sauce before serving.

Bean Sausage Soup

Ingredients

2 packages 16 bean soup
6 bay leaves
25 ml fresh oregano (chopped)
4 cans chicken stock
Additional water to cover the bean soup
6 stalks celery (chopped)
6 carrots (peeled and chopped)
2 red onions (peeled and chopped)
6 cloves garlic (minced)
2 lb chorizo sausage (sliced)
4 cans tomatoes

Method

Combine 16 bean soup, bay leaves, oregano, chicken stock together in a crock-pot.

Add enough water so that the mixture in the crock-pot is covered.

Cover the crock-pot and cook on high for 2 hours.

Add the celery, carrots, onion, garlic, sausage and tomatoes.

Cover the crock-pot.

Turn the crock-pot down to low and cook for additional 3 hours.

Bread Soup

Ingredients

4 onions (peeled and chopped)
12,5 ml butter
2 ml ground nutmeg
5 ml ground black pepper
5 ml salt
4 slices of bread
1 ½ pints water
1 ½ pints milk

Method

Sauté the onion and the butter together.

Add the nutmeg, black pepper and salt to the onion mixture.

Boil the bread in the water and milk.

Combine the onion mixture and the bread mixture together.

When the bread is tender, remove the saucepan from the heat.

Rub the mixture through a sieve.

Return the mixture to the saucepan.

Bring to boiling point and then serve.

Cabbage And Tomato Soup

Ingredients

6 green onions (chopped)
2 green peppers (seeded and chopped)
2 cans tomatoes (diced)
3 carrots (peeled and chopped)
375 ml mushrooms (sliced)
1 bunch of celery (chopped)
Half a head of cabbage (chopped)
1 package soup mix
2 cubes of beef bouillon
1 V8 juice
Salt to taste
Ground black pepper to taste
25 ml fresh parsley (chopped)
5 ml curry powder
5 ml garlic powder
3000 ml water

Method

Combine the green onions, tomatoes, green pepper together in a saucepan.

Add the cabbage, carrots, celery and mushrooms.

Add the soup mix, V8 juice, curry powder, beef bouillon cubes, salt, black pepper, fresh parsley and garlic powder.

Add the water.

Cover the saucepan.

Simmer on a low heat for 2 hours.

Caper Soup

Ingredients

3 pints water
1 ½ pints milk
18 ml capers (chopped)
Juice of ¾ lemon
3 eggs
2 ¼ oz flour
¾ oz butter
5 ml ground black pepper
10 ml salt

Method

Boil the milk, water, butter and salt and black pepper together in a saucepan.

Add the flour.

Stir until smooth.

Add the capers.

Boil the soup for 10 minutes.

Mix well.

Beat in the eggs.

Add the lemon juice.

Cauliflower Soup

Ingredients

2 cauliflowers (washed and broken into pieces)
3 pints water
62,5 ml butter
4 ml ground nutmeg
10 ml salt
10 ml ground black pepper
3 pints milk
125 ml flour
Juice of 2 lemons
Cheddar cheese (grated) for garnishing

Method

Combine the cauliflower, water, butter, nutmeg, salt and black pepper together in a saucepan.

Boil until the cauliflower is tender.

Add the milk.

Bring to the boil.

Add the flour mixed with a little water.

Stir until the soup is smooth.

Add the lemon juice.

Serve the soup in soup bowls garnished with cheddar cheese.

Chestnut Soup

Ingredients

2 lb chestnuts (unshelled)
Water to boil chestnuts
3 oz butter
25 ml flour
2 pints water
2 pints milk
50 ml fresh parsley (chopped)

Method

Place the chestnuts in cold water.

Boil the chestnuts for 60 minutes.

Remove from the heat and shell the chestnuts. Discard the water.

Sauté the chestnuts and the butter together in a pan for 10 minutes.

Add the flour while stirring all the time.

Add the water and milk.

Cook for 30 minutes.

Add the parsley.

Boil for a few minutes and then serve.

Chicken Cheese Soup

Ingredients

250 ml milk
250 ml water
2 chicken bouillon cubes
1 can cream of chicken soup
62,5 ml cheddar cheese (grated)
Salt and pepper to taste
Paprika to taste

Method

Heat the milk, water, chicken bouillon and cream of chicken soup together.

Add the cheddar cheese.

Season the soup with the salt, pepper and paprika.

Chicken Chowder

Ingredients

2 cans corn
2 cans Cream of Chicken soup
2 cans chicken broth
250 ml canned green chillies (juice included)
2 lb chicken breast (skinned and chopped into cubes)
500 ml sour cream
250 ml cheddar cheese dip

Method

Combine the corn, Cream of Chicken soup, chicken broth, green chilies together in a crock-pot.

Add the chicken.

Cover the crock-pot and cook for 3 to 4 hours.

Mix in the sour cream and cheese dip.

Stir well.

Cover the crock-pot and cook for an additional 20 minutes.

Chicken Noodle Soup

Ingredients

3 1/2 lb chicken (skinned, de-boned and cut up)
2 carrots (peeled and chopped)
125 ml onion (chopped)
2 celery stalks (chopped)
13 ml salt
190 ml parsley (chopped)
3 ml marjoram
3 ml basil
2 ml chicken seasoning
2 ml pepper
1 bay leaf
2000 ml water
625 ml egg noodles (uncooked)

Method

Combine the chicken, carrots, onion and celery together in a crock-pot.

Combine the salt, parsley, marjoram, basil, chicken seasoning, pepper and the bay leaf together.

Sprinkle over the chicken.

Add 1500 ml water.

Cover the crock-pot and cook on low setting 8 to 10 hours.

Remove the chicken and bay leaf.

Add the remaining water and the noodles.

Cover the crock-pot and cook on high for 35 minutes.

Chicken Vegetable Soup

Ingredients

     1 chicken
     500 ml carrots (peeled and chopped)
     250 ml celery (chopped)
     2 red onions (peeled ad chopped)
     250 ml rice (raw)
     1 can chicken broth
     Water – enough to cover everything
     10 ml salt
     5 ml ground black pepper
     10 ml garlic (minced)

Method

Combine the chicken, salt, black pepper, garlic and chicken broth together in a crock-pot.

Cover the crock-pot and cook on high for 3 hours.

Remove the chicken from the crock-pot.

De-bone the chicken.

Return the meat to the crock-pot.

Add the carrots, celery, onion and rice.

Mix well.

Cover the crock-pot and cook for 2 hours on Low, make sure that the rice is cooked.

Chili Butternut Soup

Ingredients

1000 g butternut (peeled, seeded and cut into chunks)
Salt water
2 packets chilli beef soup powder
1800 ml water
250 ml cream

Method

Boil the butternut in the salt water until it has softened.

Remove from the heat and drain off the water.

Combine the water and soup powder together.

Boil for 5 minutes.

Add the butternut.

Cook for 2 minutes.

Add the cream.

Mix well.

Heat until the soup is hot but not boiling.

Clam Chowder

Ingredients

13 oz canned clams
1 lb bacon (diced)
2 onions (peeled and chopped)
16 potatoes (peeled and cubed)
1500 ml water
32 ml salt
3 ml ground black pepper
2000 ml milk
100 ml corn flour

Method

Place the clams into a crock-pot.

Sauté the bacon and onions until the onions are soft and brown.

Add the bacon mixture to the crock-pot.

Add the potatoes, water, salt and black pepper to the crock-pot.

Cover the crock-pot and cook on High for 3 to 4 hours.

During the last hour, combine the milk with the cornstarch.

Add the milk mixture to the crock-pot.

Mix well.

Allow to cook for the last hour.

Coconut Soup With Rice

Ingredients

2 coconuts (grated)
5 ml mace
5 ml cinnamon
3 pints water
Juice of 1 lemon
2 eggs
30 ml flour
3 ml black pepper
5 ml salt
500 ml white rice (cooked)

Method

Combine the coconut, water, mace, cinnamon, salt and pepper together in a saucepan.

Bring to boiling point, reduce heat and simmer for 1 hour.

Strain the mixture through a sieve and then return the soup to the saucepan.

Combine the eggs, flour and lemon juice together.

Add the egg mixture to the soup.

Simmer for 5 minutes.

Serve with the rice.

Corn Chowder

Ingredients

60 ml margarine
2 onions (peeled and chopped)
6 potatoes (peeled and chopped)
5 ml curry powder
2 packets Chicken Noodle Soup
1200 ml boiling water
500 ml milk
2 x 340 g can whole kernel corn (drained)
10 ml salt
10 ml ground black pepper
25 ml parsley (chopped)

Method

Sauté the onion and margarine together.

Add the potato and curry powder.

Sauté for 5 minutes.

Add the soup powder, boiling water and milk.

Bring to the boil.

Reduce the heat.

Add the corn.

Simmer for 30 minutes.

Add the salt and black pepper.

Garnish with chopped parsley before serving.

Crab And Corn Bisque

Ingredients

1 pint crabmeat (diced)
125 ml butter (melted)
375 ml onion (peeled and chopped)
50 ml flour
1500 ml corn kernels
10 ml salt
5 ml ground black pepper
1 ½ quarts cream
187 ml green onions (peeled and sliced)
4 green onions for garnishing

Method

Combine the melted butter and onions together in a saucepan.

Sauté until the onions are translucent.

Add the flour and corn kernels.

Cook for 5 minutes.

Stir frequently.

Add the salt and black pepper.

Mix well.

Add the cream.

Lower the heat.

Cover the saucepan and cook over low heat for 20 minutes.

Stir occasionally.

Add the green onions and crabmeat.

Cover the saucepan.

Simmer over low heat for 10 minutes.

Stir once.

Serve hot.

Crab Soup

Ingredients

250 ml butter
62,5 ml onion (chopped)
5 ml celery salt
3 ml ground black pepper
475 ml cream
475 ml water
1 chicken bouillon cube dissolved in 250 ml boiling water
25 ml flour
1 lb crabmeat
25 ml fresh parsley (chopped) for garnish

Method

Sauté the onion and butter together until onion are tender.

Add the celery salt and black pepper.

Add the cream, water and bouillon mixture.

Add the flour.

Cook the mixture, stirring constantly until it has thickened.

Creamed Spinach Soup

Ingredients

600 g fresh spinach leaves (washed and chopped)
2 onions (peeled and chopped)
2 packets of cream of mushroom soup powder
1700 ml milk
250 ml cream
10 ml salt
5 ml ground black pepper
5 ml mustard powder
250 ml cheddar cheese (grated)

Method

Combine the spinach and onion together in a saucepan.

Cover with a lid and steam for a few minute (no need to add liquid).

Remove from heat a puree the spinach in a blender.

Combine the pureed spinach, soup powder, milk and cream together in a saucepan.

Simmer the mixture until it is smooth and has thickened. Stir often.

Add the salt, black pepper and mustard powder.

Mix well.

Pour the soup into oven-proof soup bowls.

Sprinkle the cheddar cheese over the top of the soup.

Place the soup bowls onto a baking sheet.

Place the baking sheet into the oven and grill until the cheese has melted.

Cream Of Tomato Soup

Ingredients

1 quart tomatoes (skinned and chopped)
2 ml soda
50 ml butter
50 ml flour
1 quart milk
12,5 ml salt
4 ml ground black pepper

Method

Place the tomatoes in a saucepan.

Stew the tomatoes slowly for 90 minutes.

Remove from the heat.

Rub the tomatoes through a sieve.

Return the tomatoes to a saucepan and heat.

Add the soda and mix well.

Melt butter in another saucepan.

Add the flour to the butter.

Mix well.

Add the milk.

Mix well.

Cook until the mixture is smooth and thick, stir constantly.

Add the salt and black pepper.

Combine the hot tomatoes and the white sauce.

Mix well.

Cullen Skink Soup

Ingredients

1 lb smoked haddock
1000 ml water
1 onion (peeled and chopped)
250 ml milk
625 ml potatoes (cooked and mashed)
2 ml ground mace
4 ml salt
3 ml ground black pepper
12,5 ml butter for serving
62,5 ml fresh parsley (chopped) for serving

Method

Combine the fish and water together in a saucepan.

Bring to the boil and immediately reduce the heat.

Simmer half covered for 10 minutes.

Remove the haddock from the saucepan.

De-bone and flake the fish.

Place the fish pieces back into the saucepan.

Add the onions.

Cover the saucepan and simmer for 20 minutes.

Heat the milk to boiling point then remove from heat.

Add the heated milk to the fish.

Simmer for a few more minutes.

Add the mashed potatoes, mace, black pepper and salt.

Heat the mixture.

Remove from the heat.

Place the butter and parsley on the top before serving.

Curried Pumpkin Soup

Ingredients

4 lb pumpkin
1 lb bacon (diced)
2 potatoes (peeled and chopped)
8 tomatoes (skinned, peeled and chopped)
4 onions (peeled and chopped)
20 ml chicken bouillon
5 ml ground black pepper
2500 ml water
15 ml curry powder
750 ml milk
250 ml cream

Method

Combine the pumpkin, bacon, potatoes, tomatoes, onions, chicken bouillon, black pepper and water together in a crock-pot.

Cover the crock-pot and cook on low for 6 hours.

Add the curry powder, milk and cream.

Cover the crock-pot.

Cook for 30 minutes on High.

Fish Chowder

Ingredients

2 lb haddock (skinned and cut into small pieces)
500 ml water
1 onion (chopped)
250 ml potatoes (peeled and sliced)
125 ml tomatoes (stewed)
7,5 ml salt
2 ml ground black pepper
25 ml butter
375 ml milk

Method

Combine the fish head, bones, skin and onion in water for 1/2 hour.

Strain the fish stock.

Combine the fish stock, potatoes, tomatoes, salt, and pepper together.

Simmer until the potatoes are soft.

Add the butter and milk.

French Onion Soup

Ingredients

75 ml oil
12 white onions (peeled and sliced)
4000 ml beef broth
500 ml water
25 ml salt
5 ml garlic powder
3 ml ground black pepper
10 hamburger buns (sliced in half)
20 slices cheese
100 ml parmesan cheese (grated)

Method

Heat the oil in saucepan.

Add the onions.

Sauté for 20 minutes.

Add the beef broth, water, salt, garlic powder and black pepper.

Bring the mixture to the boil.

Reduce heat.

Simmer for 45 minutes.

Cut all the bun pieces the same size, but make them as large as possible and place on a baking sheet.

Preheat the oven to 325 degrees F.

Bake at 325 degrees F for 15 to 20 minutes.

Set the large croutons aside.

When serving the soup pour the soup into oven-safe bowls.

Float a crouton on top of each bowl of soup.

Place a slice of cheese on top of the crouton and sprinkle a little parmesan cheese on top.

Place the bowls of soup onto a baking sheet and place in the oven.

Broil the soup for 5 to 6 minutes or until the cheese is melted and starting to brown.

Sprinkle additional parmesan cheese over the top of the soup and serve.

Hungarian Goulash Soup

Ingredients

2 lb steak (chopped into cubes)
250 ml onion (peeled and chopped)
1 clove garlic (chopped)
25 ml flour
5 ml salt
3 ml ground black pepper
7,5 ml paprika
3 ml thyme
1000 ml water
1 can tomatoes
250 ml sour cream

Method

Combine the steak cubes, onion and garlic together in a crock-pot.

Stir in the flour.

Mix well to coat the steak cubes.

Add the salt, black pepper, paprika, thyme, water and tomatoes.

Mix well.

Cover the crock-pot and cook on LOW for 8 to 10 hours.

Stir occasionally.

Add sour cream 30 minutes before serving.

Lentil Soup

Ingredients

2 lb lentils (washed)
2 lb potatoes (peeled and chopped)
2 onions (chopped)
2 heads celery (chopped)
1 lb tomatoes
62,5 ml butter
5 ml ground black pepper
10 ml salt
4 quarts chicken stock

Method

Sauté the onion and butter together.

Combine the lentils and chicken stock together in a saucepan.

Add the onion, celery and potatoes.

When the lentils are nearly soft add the tomatoes.

Add the black pepper and salt.

Add more water if the soup is too thick.

Lobster Bisque Soup Recipe

Ingredients

2 lb lobsters (boiled and diced)
625 ml chicken stock
1 onion (peeled and chopped)
4 celery stalks (chopped)
2 whole cloves
1 bay leaf
62,5 ml butter
62,5 ml flour
750 ml milk (heated)
2 ml ground nutmeg
250 ml cream (hot)
25 ml sherry
2 ml parsley (chopped)
2 ml paprika

Method

Combine the chicken stock, onion, celery, cloves and bay leaf together in a saucepan.

Simmer for 15 minutes.

Remove from the heat.

Strain the stock.

Combine the flour and butter together in a saucepan.

Simmer for 5 minutes.

Add the heated milk.

Whisk to combine thoroughly.

Add the nutmeg.

Add the chicken stock mixture.

Cook the soup until the mixture is smooth.

Add the lobster.

Allow the bisque to simmer.

Add the sherry.

Cover the saucepan for 5 minutes while simmering.

Turn off the heat.

Stir in the cream.

Mango Soup

Ingredients

    3 mangoes (chopped fine)
1500 ml chicken soup stock
37,5 ml lemon grass
37,5 ml ginger (chopped)
10 ml ground chili peppers
750 ml yogurt
75 ml cilantro (chopped)

Method

Combine the mangoes, ginger, lemon grass, chili and 125 ml soup stock together.

Blend until smooth.

Combine the mango mixture and the remaining chicken stock.

Mix well.

Add the yogurt.

Mix well.

Serve the soup cold.

Mushroom Soup

Ingredients

25 ml butter (melted)
500 ml carrots (peeled and diced)
250 ml green onions (sliced)
10 ml garlic (minced)
5 ml salt
3 ml thyme
3 ml ground black pepper
3 lb white mushrooms (sliced)
2 cans chicken broth
500 ml white wine
750 ml milk

Method

Combine the butter, carrots, onions, garlic, salt, thyme and black pepper together in a saucepan.

Simmer for 5 minutes.

Stir often.

Add the mushrooms, chicken broth and wine.

Bring to the boil.

Cook for 1 minute.

Remove 250 ml of the vegetables and set aside.

Pour the soup into a blender and puree the mixture.

Return the pureed mixture to the saucepan.

Add the milk and reserved vegetables.

Simmer for 5 minutes.

Serve hot.

Onion Soup

Ingredients

3 lb onions (peeled and chopped)
1 stick butter
2 cans beef broth
250 ml water

Method

Combine all the ingredients together in a crock-pot.

Cover the crock-pot and cook on Low for 6 hours.

Parsnip Soup

Ingredients

6 parsnips (peeled and chopped)
2 onions (peeled and chopped)
2 sticks celery (chopped)
1 oz butter
2 quarts water
5 ml ground black pepper
10 ml salt
1 pint milk
25 ml flour
25 ml vinegar

Method

Combine the parsnips, onions, celery, butter, water, salt and black pepper together in a crock-pot.

Cover the crock-pot and cook on low for 3 to 4 hours.

Add the milk and flour.

Boil for 5 minutes.

Switch off heat.

Add the vinegar.

Pea Soup

Ingredients

2 kg pork
500 ml onion (peeled and chopped)
200 ml celery (chopped)
2 bay leaves
3 ml thyme
50 ml salt
10 ml ground black pepper
1000 g dried split peas
4500 ml water

Method

Combine all the ingredients together into a crock-pot.

Cover the crock-pot.

Cook on Low for 4 to 5 hours.

Pea Soup With Dumplings

Ingredients

6 leeks (topped and sliced)
4 carrots (peeled and chopped)
750 ml peas
2000 ml chicken stock
15 ml salt
5 ml paprika
25 ml oil
500 ml flour
2 eggs
125 ml butter
5 ml dried mixed herbs
Little water

Method

Sauté the oil, leeks, carrots and peas together in a saucepan.

Pour the stir fried vegetables into a crock-pot.

Add the chicken stock.

Combine the eggs and butter together.

Add the flour and mixed herbs.

Mix well.

Add a little water to make soft dough.

Spoon the dumplings into the soup.

Cover the crock-pot and cook on low heat for 6 – 8 hours.

Potato And Sweet Chili Soup

Ingredients

1 kg potatoes (peeled and chopped)
750 ml water
20 ml salt
5 ml ground black pepper
3 red onions (peeled and chopped)
500 g pork neck (chopped into cubes)
125 ml sweet chili sauce
1 packet Thai chili sauce powder

Method

Combine the potatoes, water, salt, black pepper, onions, pork neck, Thai chili sauce powder and sweet chili sauce together in a saucepan.

Cook until the potatoes are very soft.

Remove from the heat.

Mash the potatoes fine with a potato masher.

Potato And Zucchini Soup

Ingredients

1 kg pork neck (chopped into cubes)
2500 ml chicken stock
2kg potatoes (peeled and chopped)
2kg zucchini (sliced)
4 onions (peeled and chopped)
5 ml ground nutmeg
25 ml natural yoghurt

Method

Combine the pork neck, chicken stock, potatoes, zucchini, onions, nutmeg and yogurt into the crock-pot.

Cover the crock-pot and cook for 8-10 hours on Low.

Rice Soup

Ingredients

90 ml rice
2 1/2 pints water
125 ml cheddar cheese (grated)
250 ml tomato juice
30 ml butter
3 ml black pepper
5 ml salt

Method

Boil the rice and water together.

When the rice is tender add the butter, salt and pepper.

Boil until the rice is quite soft then add the tomato juice and the cheese.

Stir cheese has dissolved.

If too much of the water has boiled away add a little more water.

Rice And Onion Soup

Ingredients

8 onions (peeled and chopped)
6 oz of rice
3 oz butter
6 pints water
5 ml ground black pepper
5 ml salt

Method

Combine all the ingredients together in a crock-pot.

Cover the crock-pot and cook on low for 3 to 4 hours.

Salsa And Black Bean Soup

Ingredients

2 cans black beans
375 ml chicken stock
250 ml salsa
5 ml ground cumin
62,5 ml sour cream
2 green onions (chopped)

Method

Combine the beans, salsa, cumin and chicken stock together in a blender.

Puree the mixture.

Pour the mixture into a saucepan.

Heat the mixture until boiling point.

Stir in the onions and sour cream.

Scotch Broth

Ingredients

1lb neck of mutton
25 ml pearl barley
12,5 ml coarse oatmeal
62,5 ml dried peas
Water to soak barley and oatmeal
2 quarts water
1 turnip (diced)
1 carrot (grated)
1 leek (sliced)
1 onion (diced)
25 ml parsley (chopped)
Small piece of cabbage
125 ml brown portion of crust of loaf of whole wheat bread (cut into small pieces)
Salt to season
250 ml milk
125 ml cream

Method

Soak the pearl barley, dried peas and oatmeal in water overnight.

Combine the mutton, barley, oatmeal, water in which they were soaked and 2 quarts water together in a saucepan.

Simmer for several hours.

Add boiling water as needed.

Add the turnip, carrot, onion, leek, parsley, cabbage and pieces of crust.

Simmer for 1 more hour.

Remove from the heat and rub the broth through a colander.

Add the salt, milk and cream.

Seafood Chowder

Ingredients

250 g bacon (diced)
2 onions (peeled and chopped)
900 g potatoes (peeled and chopped)
900 g fish fillets (chopped into chunks)
3200 ml milk
1200 ml water
2 bay leaves
25 ml Worcestershire sauce

Method

Sauté the bacon until 5 minutes.

Add the potato.

Sauté for 5 minutes.

Add the onions.

Sauté for 5 minutes.

Place into a crock-pot.

Add fish.

Add the milk, water, bay leaves and Worcestershire sauce.

Cover the crock-pot and cook on low for about 5 hours.

Squash Soup

Ingredients

    1 onion (peeled and chopped)
125 ml shallots (minced)
500 ml carrots (peeled and grated)
1500 ml butternut squash (seeded, peeled and chopped)
25 ml butter
1 bay leaf
2 Granny Smith apples (peeled, cored and chopped)
5 ml curry powder
125 ml water
1000 ml chicken broth
125 ml sour cream
5 ml salt
4 ml ground black pepper
Water

Method

Sauté the onion, shallots, carrots and bay leaf in the butter until the onion has softened.

Add the squash, apple, chicken broth and water.

Mix well.

Add the curry powder, salt and pepper.

Simmer for 45 minutes.

Remove from the heat.

Remove the bay leaf.

Pour the soup into a blender and puree the soup.

Transfer the soup to a clean saucepan.

Add enough additional water to thin soup to desired consistency.

Serve with sour cream.

Sweet Potato And Lentil Soup

Ingredients

25 ml olive oil
2 onions (peeled and chopped)
4 celery sticks (sliced)
2 red peppers (seeded and chopped)
2 sweet potatoes (peeled and chopped)
50 ml garlic (minced)
25 ml ground cumin
25 ml salt
25 ml ground black pepper
10 ml onion powder
10 ml oregano
10 ml chilli pepper
500 ml lentils
250 ml Quinoa
3000 ml beef stock

Method

Combine all the ingredients together in a crock pot.

Blend well.

Cover the crock-pot and cook on medium heat for 6 hours.

Tomato And Basil Soup

Ingredients

2 kg tomatoes (skinned and chopped)
1 kg pork neck
25 ml olive oil
Bunch of fresh basil (chopped)
50 ml pesto
20 ml salt
10 ml ground black pepper

Method

Sauté the pork neck and the olive oil together until the pork has browned.

Combine the tomatoes, basil, pesto, salt and black pepper together in a saucepan.

Add the pork.

Mix well.

Cook the mixture over a low heat until the tomatoes are very soft (no liquid is required as the tomatoes make enough liquid on their own).

Vegetable Soup

Ingredients

625 ml pinto beans (soaked overnight and drained
– throw this liquid away)
Water to cover beans when cooking
10 ml salt
1 bay leaf
10 ml dried oregano
2 lb tomatoes (peeled, seeded and chopped)
4 chilies (seeded and chopped)
2 lb mixed summer squash (peeled, seeded and
chopped)
1000 ml corn kernels
10 ml ground cumin
5 ml ground coriander
50 ml oil
4 red onions (peeled and chopped)
4 cloves garlic (chopped)
20 ml red chili powder
500 ml fresh green beans (chopped)
250 ml sharp cheese (grated)
1 bunch cilantro (chopped)

Method

Combine the soaked beans, enough water to cover the
beans, bay leaf, oregano and salt together in a saucepan.

Cook for 2 hours.

Remove from the heat.

Drain the beans but save the bean stock.

Heat the oil in a saucepan.

Add the onions and sauté for 2 minutes.

Lower the heat.

Add the garlic, chili powder, cumin and coriander.

Stir well.

Add a little bean stock reserved from cooking the beans.

Simmer for 5 minutes.

Add the squash, corn kernels, green beans, chilli, cooked beans and enough bean stock to make the soup the correct consistency.

Simmer for 20 minutes.

Adjust the seasoning.

Add the cheese and cilantro.

Serve hot.

Zucchini Soup

Ingredients

1000 ml zucchini (topped, tailed and chopped)
6 tomatoes (skinned and chopped)
2 onions (peeled and chopped)
15 ml salt
10 ml ground black pepper
25 ml parsley (chopped)
25 ml basil
75 ml oil
500 ml macaroni
2750 ml beef stock (boiling)

Method

Sauté the oil and onion together.

Add the zucchini and tomatoes.

Stir constantly.

Place the onion mixture into a crock-pot.

Add the beef stock.

Cover the crock-pot and cook on low heat for 2 hours

Add the macaroni, parsley, basil, salt and black pepper.

Cover the crock-pot and cook for 1 hour on high heat

Zucchini And Apple Soup

Ingredients

20 ml curry powder
2000 ml chicken stock
1400 g zucchini (topped and sliced)
4 apples (peeled, cored and chopped)
4 onions (peeled and chopped)
250 ml bacon (diced and fried)
75 ml cream per serving

Method

Combine the curry powder and chicken stock together.

Place the zucchini, apples and onions into the crock-pot.

Pour the chicken stock over the vegetables.

Cover the crock-pot and cook for 8-10 hours on Low.

Add the fried bacon.

Mix well.

Pour the soup into soup bowls.

Add the cream per serving just before serving.

Made in the USA
San Bernardino, CA
21 August 2015